Writing Teacher's Han[d]
Narrative Writing

Written by June Hetzel and Deborah McIntire

"When we have something to say
and the words are on the tip of our pens to say it,
what power we unleash!"
—Mauree Applegate

from *Slithery Snakes and Other Aides to Children's Writings*
by Walter T. Petty and Mary E. Bowen. Prentice-Hall, Inc. 1967.

Illustrator: Corbin Hillam
Editor: Joel Kupperstein
Project Director: Carolea Williams

Table of Contents

Introduction 3

Writing Domains

Lesson Plan Format

The Writing Process 4

Prewriting

Rough Draft

Revising

Editing

Publishing/Presenting

Writing Devices 10

Alliteration

Metaphor

Simile

Sensory Detail

Onomatopoeia

Personification

Assessment 12

Writing Process Cards . . 13

Editing Marks 14

Writing Lessons

Autobiographical
Incident 15

Ballad 23

Biographical Sketch 29

Short Story 35

Fable 43

Fairy Tale 50

Tall Tale 57

Bibliography 64

Introduction

Narrative Writing is one resource in the *Writing Teacher's Handbook* four-book series that assists teachers of grades 4–6 in effectively implementing classroom writing programs. The lessons in each book include actual writing samples from upper-grade students.

Writing Domains

Each resource book in the *Writing Teacher's Handbook* series describes detailed lessons in one of the four writing domains—narrative, expressive, informative, and persuasive.

The *narrative domain* focuses on telling a story (e.g., autobiographical incidents, short stories). The *expressive domain* includes poems and stories that express sensory detail and emotions (e.g., journal entries, haiku). The *persuasive domain* involves convincing readers of beliefs and reasoning (e.g., persuasive essays, editorial comments). The *informative domain* encompasses writing products that explain factual information (e.g., research papers, reports).

Many writing products fall within more than one domain. For example, a ballad describes a person's emotions (expressive) but also tells a story (narrative). A dialogue can evoke emotion (expressive), but can also comprise the content of an interview (informative). Emphasize the critical components of each writing product to help your students sharpen their writing skills and prepare them for writing success.

Lesson Plan Format

Lessons in this book include:

Critical Components—a list of the essential components of each writing product

Preparation—a description of what teachers need to do prior to the lesson

Setting the Stage—hints for introducing the lesson and engaging student interest

Instructional Input—directions for initiating a formal writing lesson and modeling the critical components of writing samples

Guided Practice—exercises for reinforcing the writing lesson

Independent Practice—activities to help students write independently

Presentation—ideas for organizing, publishing, and presenting student work

Teaching Hints/Extensions—tips to explore and extend the topic and writing domain

In addition, at the end of each section is a reproducible rubric for evaluating student work. Give students the rubric at the beginning of the lesson so they can write with specific goals in mind.

The Writing Process

The writing process involves five steps: prewriting, writing a rough draft, revising, editing, and publishing/presenting the final product. These five steps are integral to any type of writing and form the foundation for all writing lessons in this book. Guide students through the stages of the process for each writing lesson, particularly the activities in the Independent Practice sections. Emphasize to students that they may need to repeat the cycle of revising and editing several times until their manuscript is ready for publication. Provide students with copies of the Writing Process Cards (page 13), and have them complete a card for each writing task and attach it to the final product. The first space for check-off in the Editing box of the Writing Process Card is for self-editing and the second is for peer or teacher editing.

Prewriting

Prewriting occurs after a thorough discussion of a topic but before formal writing about the topic. The prewriting stage is a structured brainstorming session aimed at eliciting spontaneous thinking about a specific topic. During the prewriting stage, help students use clusters and graphic organizers to organize their thoughts. For example, prewriting for a paragraph about how upset James was with his brother might include a simple cluster such as the following.

The central idea, James' feelings, becomes the basis for the topic sentence. The content of the cluster's spokes becomes the basis for supporting sentences.

Most of the lessons in this book pertain to various types of stories. When writing stories, encourage students to plan how they will catch the reader's attention with a strong beginning, build tension or momentum as they move to the climax of the story, and bring resolution at the conclusion of the story. A flow chart such as the following can assist students in prewriting planning.

Throughout this book, you will find graphic organizers that help students organize their thinking and include the critical components in each of their writing products.

After students complete the brainstorming session, they should skim over their prewriting work and trim unnecessary or irrelevant content. The remaining information will form the skeleton or framework of the project.

Rough Draft

The rough draft is the first round of organized writing. During rough-draft writing, students write spontaneously, following the organizational framework of the prewriting graphic organizer. Students should feel free to deviate from the skeletal framework of the prewriting organizer, as long as the requirements of the writing type (as defined by the rubric) are met. Frequently, the most creative writing comes from the spontaneity of a rough draft.

Students should not worry about precise spelling and punctuation while writing rough drafts. During the editing stage, however, spelling and punctuation should be fine-tuned to perfection!

Revising

The revising stage requires students to reorganize at four levels: the entire piece, each paragraph (or stanza), each sentence (or line), and each individual word. Encourage students to revise in this order to save time and, potentially, unnecessary work. For example, if a writer deletes an entire paragraph, no time is wasted revising the sentences or words in that paragraph.

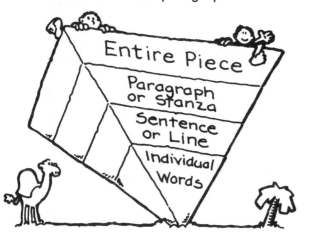

Revising the Entire Piece

At this level of revising, students look at the "big picture." They read and reread their writing, asking the following questions.

Does the piece flow from one idea to another?

Are paragraphs or stanzas in a logical sequence?

Are there transitions between paragraphs or stanzas?

Is the writing clear and understandable?

Does the writing product meet the requirements of the rubric?

Does the piece contain sensory detail?

Is this a well-told story?

Does this story have a beginning, a middle, and an end?

Are the setting, characters, and conflict clear?

Does this story have a strong beginning that pulls the reader into the story?

Does this story contain suspense, curiosity, or tension that builds up to the climax?

Does this story have a strong ending that includes a resolution, surprise ending, or twist?

Revising Each Paragraph or Stanza

In addition to larger organizational revising, students must revise their writing at the paragraph or stanza level. At this stage, students carefully examine each paragraph, asking the following:

For prose—

Are sentences arranged in logical order?

Is there a topic sentence?

Are there supporting sentences?

Have I avoided redundancy?

Does each paragraph add to the clarity, depth, and/or intensity of the piece?

For poetry—

Does the main idea flow through each stanza?

Does the main emotion flow through each stanza?

Are lines effectively sequenced?

Does each stanza add to the clarity, depth, and/or intensity of the piece?

Writing Tip

It is common for beginning writers to struggle with the sentence order of a paragraph. Model the following "cut-and-paste" methods to demonstrate how to revise a paragraph.
1. Cut and paste using the computer.
2. Physically cut and paste the text to different sections of the page.
3. Color-code sentences that belong together.

Revising Each Sentence or Line

Students may wish to reorder or revise words within sentences (or lines) to strengthen the meaning conveyed to the reader as well as to add interest.

Weak Example:
I felt bad about the situation.

Strong Example:
My eyes swelled with tears over the situation.

Word efficiency is another aspect of sentence revision. Students should be taught to use as few as words as necessary to relay the desired meaning.

Weak Example:
The wood cabinet made of mahogany was beautiful, and we decided to buy it.

Strong Example:
We decided to buy the beautiful mahogany cabinet.

Revising Individual Words

Revising at the word level constitutes fine-tuning. This is the time to have students pull out the thesaurus and dictionary. This is the time to polish!

Here are some tips for revising at the word level:

Use interesting words—

>Weak Example:
>**The decorated shirt was pretty.**

>Strong Example:
>**The rhinestone-studded vest dazzled everyone.**

Strengthen verbs—

>Weak Example:
>**She ate her dinner.**

>Strong Example:
>**She devoured her dinner.**

Clarify pronouns—

>Weak Example:
>**He met him at the park.**

>Strong Example:
>**Mr. Felig met Jonathan at the park.**

Clarify vague concepts—

>Weak Example:
>**Mr. Felig and Jonathan played a game.**

>Strong Example:
>**Mr. Felig and Jonathan played polo.**

Use sensory detail to evoke emotion—

>Weak Example:
>**She was sad.**

>Strong Example:
>**She couldn't hide her tear-stained cheeks and muffled sobs.**

Editing

At the editing stage, students make sure words are spelled correctly and punctuation is accurate. Here are some hints for this ongoing area of growth.

Editing Marks

Photocopy the Editing Marks reproducible (page 14) for students to refer to as they complete this stage of the writing process. Be sure students are familiar with and comfortable using editing symbols before beginning their first writing-process piece.

Spelling

Have students keep ongoing personal dictionaries in which they record new words they encounter. Included in these dictionaries should be a list of the most commonly used words in their writing. Also, be sure students have access to comprehensive dictionaries and thesauruses. Reinforce the idea that students may need to repeat the editing stage for any particular writing project.

If your students write using a computer, teach them how to use programs that check spelling. However, be sure that they clearly understand that computers will not detect missing words or homophone errors.

Punctuation

Mastering punctuation can be challenging. Teach punctuation as you teach writing, starting with the basics (ending punctuation and capitalization) and moving to commas, semicolons, and colons as students gain mastery. Do not expect perfection at the rough-draft stage. The goal of teaching writing is to help students improve their writing with each revision.

Repeated Reading

Students often have the misconception that one round of reading is sufficient in editing a piece. Encourage several reads by several people (the author, peers, and adults). Each reading provides an opportunity to improve the writing. For peer editing, students might engage in a round robin discussion or an "author's chair," where one student reads a piece to the group or class and solicits constructive feedback.

Publishing/Presenting

The most rewarding aspect of the writing process is the final draft, or publishing/presenting stage. At this point, the writer finally sees his or her completed work in polished form, available for others' enjoyment. Provide forums for students to read their writing to one another, to other classes, and to parents. Encourage students to bind their writing into books and submit copies to school and classroom libraries. Students may also want to submit their work to local newspapers for publication. Tape-record stories for reading centers and post students' writing in your classroom on bulletin board displays.

Writing Devices

Certain literary devices can increase the effectiveness and beauty of students' writing. These devices include alliteration, metaphor, simile, sensory detail, onomatopoeia, and personification. Review these devices throughout your writing lessons, particularly during the revising stage. Challenge students to locate these devices in their independent reading materials.

Alliteration

Increase students' understanding of how alliteration—a string of words with the same initial sound—enhances the "sound" of language. Read and recite classic tongue twisters *(Peter Piper picked a peck of pickled peppers),* make up original tongue twisters *(Rhonda Rhino wrestled raggedy Rita Rhino),* and brainstorm phrases that include repetitive initial sounds *(Sally's savory sweets, Dominating Dominic, Veronica Victor's venom).* Challenge students to complete these alliterative phrases and use alliteration in their writing. The use of alliteration is especially effective in poetry such as quatrains and limericks, where an author composes poetic phrases that evoke mental images and have auditory appeal because of the sound repetition.

Metaphor

Increase students' ability to relay meaning to a reader by comparing two ideas using "word pictures," or metaphors. Read some ordinary sentences and enhance the meaning of the sentences by rewriting them using metaphors.

Weak Example:
The manuscript has a lot of good qualities and can be improved.

Strong Example:
The manuscript is a diamond in the rough.

Weak Example:
The young man is very strong and one day will be in the Olympics.

Strong Example:
Such a young Hercules will one day compete in the Olympics.

Simile

Similar to metaphor, a simile compares two ideas using *as* or *like*. Help students enjoy similes by reading *Quick As a Cricket* by Audrey Wood. Discuss simile examples in the book, such as *quick as a cricket* and *strong as an ox*. Discuss how similes evoke images that enhance the mental pictures of what the writer is trying to relate.

Sensory Detail

Writers who use sensory detail (words and phrases that vividly describe sight, sound, smell, taste, and touch) involve the reader's senses and add interest to their writing.

Weak Example:
I felt hot and tired after the race through the desert.

Strong Example:
Every inch of my body ached after the grueling race through the scorching, arid desert.

Onomatopoeia

Onomatopoeic words represent the sounds of the things they describe, for example, *crunch, crackle,* and *bang.* These words help clarify readers' mental images and intensify events and emotions.

Weak Example:
I heard a loud sound come from next door.

Strong Example:
Bang! The explosive sound pierced the air.

Weak Example:
The magician made the object disappear.

Strong Example:
Poof! With a wave of the magician's wand, the object disappeared.

Personification

Personification is the assigning of human characteristics to a nonhuman object or animal. To provide students practice with this device, guide them in brainstorming a list of objects and the human characteristics that could describe them. Then, create sentences using items from this personification list. For example, students might use the word *shy* to describe the moon. Then, they might write the sentence *The moon peeked shyly through the clouds.*

Assessment

Each lesson in this resource includes a rubric for evaluating student work. These rubrics allow readers to assess the critical components, style issues, originality, and mechanics of the work. Some also include space for readers' comments.

Rubrics are valuable tools at all stages of the writing process. Give the rubrics to students as they begin prewriting to help them understand the criteria by which their work will be assessed. At this early stage, rubrics also help students understand the focus and purpose of each writing genre.

As students revise their own work, rubrics help them assess the quality of what they have written. Have students complete a rubric for each draft they write and include detailed comments each time. Also, have peer editors complete rubrics when evaluating classmates' work. Objectively evaluating one's own work is a difficult task, to be sure. Give students practice evaluating each other's work. When students make tactful, constructive comments, they contribute to the improvement of each other's writing.

Rubrics also give you a standardized format for the final assessment of students' writing. Ask students to attach all of their completed rubrics to each project they turn in. Use the student-completed rubrics to assess the progress students made while writing.

When you complete the final rubric and present it to students, they will clearly understand why they received the grades they were given.

As students complete writing projects, you may want to store their work in portfolios. Whether your portfolios are simple file folders in a file cabinet or decorated pizza boxes in which students can store artwork that accompanies their writing, be sure students have open access to them. Invite students to add at any time work they feel shows growth or excellence. Review these portfolios when determining students' writing grades, and have them available for parents to look through at Open House and at parent-teacher conferences.

Writing Process Cards

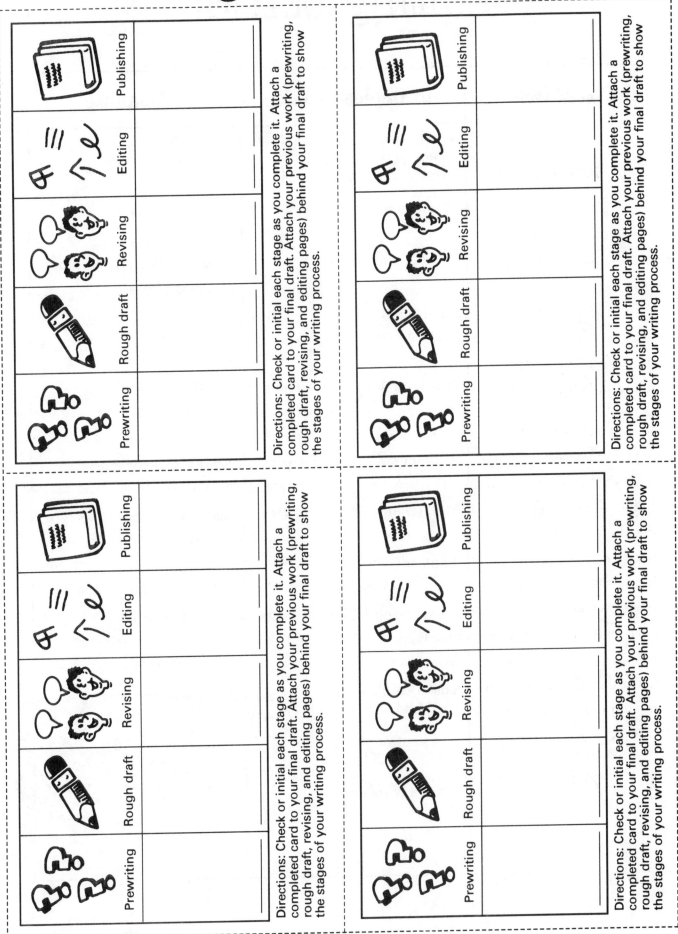

Prewriting	Rough draft	Revising	Editing	Publishing

Directions: Check or initial each stage as you complete it. Attach a completed card to your final draft. Attach your previous work (prewriting, rough draft, revising, and editing pages) behind your final draft to show the stages of your writing process.

Prewriting	Rough draft	Revising	Editing	Publishing

Directions: Check or initial each stage as you complete it. Attach a completed card to your final draft. Attach your previous work (prewriting, rough draft, revising, and editing pages) behind your final draft to show the stages of your writing process.

Prewriting	Rough draft	Revising	Editing	Publishing

Directions: Check or initial each stage as you complete it. Attach a completed card to your final draft. Attach your previous work (prewriting, rough draft, revising, and editing pages) behind your final draft to show the stages of your writing process.

Prewriting	Rough draft	Revising	Editing	Publishing

Directions: Check or initial each stage as you complete it. Attach a completed card to your final draft. Attach your previous work (prewriting, rough draft, revising, and editing pages) behind your final draft to show the stages of your writing process.

Editing Marks

Editing Mark	Examples in Text	Meaning
≡	watch out!	Capitalize the letter.
/	Come here Quickly.	Use lowercase.
^	Look at that girafe. (f inserted)	Insert a letter. (This symbol is called a caret.)
⊙	Place a period here ⊙	Insert a period.
^ (with comma)	When it rains the geraniums love it.	Insert a comma.
¶	. . . with me. ¶ The next day . . .	Start a new paragraph.
“ ”	Good morning, Sally called.	Insert quotations.
⁀‿	pop corn	Join words.
(delete mark)	June and and Deborah wrote this book.	Delete this word.
^	Luella Carolea like it. (and inserted)	Insert a word.
(reverse mark)	Can you with come me?	Reverse word order.
#	Make a wisedecision.	Insert a space.

Narrative Writing © 1998 Creative Teaching Press

Autobiographical Incident

Critical Components

An autobiographical incident describes a single event in first person. An autobiographical incident describes the event in sequential order, including a beginning, a middle, and an end. An autobiographical incident incorporates vivid description and sensory detail.

Preparation

Think of a personal autobiographical incident to share with the class. Bring in several short stories. Choose a few stories that are clear examples of third-person writing and a few that are clear examples of first-person writing. Make an overhead transparency of page 18. Photocopy pages 19–22 for students.

Setting the Stage

Share with the class that everyone has many autobiographical incidents in their lives—some are funny, some are scary, some are happy, and some are sad. Tell the class about an autobiographical incident of your own. After describing the incident, ask students to retell the story. List the major events in chronological order on the board. Then, ask if anyone else has an autobiographical incident to share. Give each volunteer a few minutes to tell his or her story.

Instructional Input

1. Explain to students that an autobiographical incident is written in first person, using the pronoun "I"—in the same way their classmates just shared their stories.

2. Read the first paragraph or two of the stories you brought in, and ask students to identify whether or not the story is told in first or third person.

3. Once students understand the difference between first- and third-person storytelling, introduce the idea of sequential order. List several events on the board, such as

   I ate breakfast and packed my lunch.
   I walked to school.
   I gave my teacher my absence note.
   I woke up.

4. Ask students to arrange the events in the order they would likely have occurred. Stress that a well-written autobiographical incident includes a beginning, a middle, and an end.

5. Using an overhead transparency of page 18, bracket the beginning, middle, and end sections of the story to stress these larger components.

6. Next, introduce vivid description and sensory detail. Ask students to rewrite the following bland sentences:
   Charlie drank the water.
   Sharon was upset.

   Rewritten sentences might look something like this:
   Charlie guzzled the cool water while sweat dripped from his brow.
   Sharon trembled with anger when she saw the unjust treatment of her little brother.

Guided Practice

1. Invite the class to read the student-authored autobiographical incidents on pages 19 and 20. Ask them to identify the key components of an autobiographical incident and respond to the discussion questions at the bottom of each page.

2. Have students think of an exciting event that really happened to them, such as a birthday party, an accomplishment they are proud of, or a memorable outing.

3. Ask students to use the Autobiographical Incident Frame on page 21 to organize their autobiographical incidents. This is the prewriting stage of the writing process.

Independent Practice

1. After students have completed the frame, have them write a rough draft. Have them submit the draft to you or to a classmate for preliminary assessment using the Autobiographical Incident Rubric on page 22.

2. Ask evaluators to encourage revision of the rough drafts by identifying bland writing phrases and changing them to vivid writing that includes sensory detail. For example:

   Bland Example:
   I walked up to Disneyland.

   Vivid Example:
   Nervous with excitement, I charged up to Disneyland's entrance, unaware of the crowds around me.

   Bland Example:
   I hit my head on the sidewalk.

   Vivid Example:
   Tripping on the curb in front of the Lincoln Memorial, I fell and smacked my head on the concrete sidewalk.

Presentation

- Compile writings in a class book titled *It Happened on _____ Street.* (Insert the street name of your school.)

- Have students cut outlines of their bodies from butcher paper. Then, have them illustrate self-portraits and attach the portraits to the head of the cutout. Glue students' autobiographical incidents to the outline's torso, and display the finished products around the room.

Teaching Hints/Extensions

- Telling oral stories is common practice in many cultures. Invite extended-family members to visit the class and tell stories about their family's past.

- Challenge students to rewrite their autobiographical incidents in a puppet-play or skit format and perform them for the class.

- Invite students to write a chronological series of autobiographical incidents. Have them compile these incidents into a complete autobiography. This makes a great yearlong project to display at Open House.

THE BIG DAY

Autobiographical Incident
Sample 1

• My Two Chipped Teeth •

Student Author: Andrew Kuhl

I really used to like to ride my skateboard down the hill in front of my house. One day, my friend André and I decided to take turns riding the skateboard on the slanted patio.

It was André's turn to ride down, and I rode the skateboard up the patio to him. I kneeled with one knee on the skateboard and used the other foot to push myself up. One brick on the patio stuck out about half an inch.

I said to myself, "It's an easy jump." I prepared to lift the front wheels of my skateboard, but I was too late. I flew off the skateboard and hit the ground really hard with my face. Instantly, my lips swelled up and I could taste the blood in my mouth. I was scared and asked André, "Are my teeth okay?"

He said I had chipped off both of my front teeth. We had to go to the dentist. The dentist took many X-rays to see if the teeth were fractured. I was lucky again; they were not.

A few weeks later the dentist fixed the damage. My mom bit her lips and paid the bill. I don't ride my skateboard much anymore.

Narrative Writing © 1998 Creative Teaching Press

Autobiographical Incident
Sample 2

• My Dream •

Student Author: Joanne Johnson

Being a young ballet dancer, I had a dream of getting a solo or a main part in a ballet. My ballet instructor offered me a solo in the summer performance at the Fullerton College Theater. I was very exuberant about her decision. I practiced hard every day for two weeks. I rehearsed at my dance studio, under my teacher's instruction.

On the day of the performance, I felt good physically and mentally, and I knew I was prepared to do well. Before the performance began, I stretched and reviewed my number on the stage. When I put on my makeup and costume, I felt nervous with anticipation.

As I stepped onto the stage I had a new feeling. I would be dancing all alone for the first time. My number was called "Czech Sketches," featuring music by Bedrich Smetana. Finally, it was my turn to go out and perform. I took a deep breath and closed my eyes, thinking about my dance. Then, I made my entrance with confident thoughts.

The stage was blacked out, so no one could see me entering. I stepped into the center of the stage and waited for the music to begin. Then, the gentle music started and the spotlight was on me. I did my dance steps and saw the audience before me. A smile was on my face, telling the audience I was enjoying this moment.

I soon came to the most difficult step in the dance. I had rehearsed this particular step at the studio, because I had had trouble with it. But, without making any mistakes, I danced completely through the whole number. The music was flowing throughout my body, and with my arms lifting through the air, I danced gracefully. Toward the end of the dance, I did my last jump and took my final pose. After it was all completed, I took my bows. The applause made me really happy, and I felt superb for performing well.

I was proud of my first solo, and I hope I have an opportunity to do it again. I received many compliments and flowers from my friends and family after the show. Even my instructor said I did well. After the performance, I felt I had improved my dancing. Younger dancers now look up to me. I had climbed another step in my ballet training. This event was a very special memory that I'll keep as my treasure.

Discussion:

1. What event does the author describe?

2. Identify the beginning, middle, and end of the story.

3. List examples in the story of vivid description and sensory detail.

Autobiographical Incident
Sample 3

• Swimming the Pier •

Student Author: Nathan Thompson

This summer in the Junior Lifeguards program, I participated in a very challenging and exciting event—swimming around the Huntington Beach Pier. Junior Lifeguards is a lifeguard training program for boys and girls 9–17 years old. The program consists of fun, challenging activities, such as two-mile runs, sand sprints, body surfing, First Aid, and simulated rescues, but the event that my friends and I anticipated the most was the pier swim. Mr. Morita, our instructor, explained how to take high steps when entering the water, to dive under the waves with your hands in front, and then to swim freestyle around the pier. This would be approximately a one-mile swim. To reassure some of the kids who were nervous, Mr. Morita told us that Safety Aides, who are graduated Junior Lifeguards, would be all around the pier with buoys on which swimmers could rest.

Finally, the day of the pier swim arrived. It was a cold day, and the water was even colder. Some of the kids were nervous, but I was not. We lined up at the starting line and when our instructor said, "Go!" we took off. I lifted my knees high to run through the water and then dove under the waves, so as not to get pushed back. When I first touched the water it was very cold and tasted salty and dirty, but I still swam. While we were swimming, people threw roses from the pier and cheered for us. Mr. Morita was on his paddleboard saying, "Let's go!" Finally, I reached the end of the pier, but I was only half done. A Safety Aide asked if I wanted to rest. Even though my arms hurt and I was out of breath, I shook my head to the Safety Aide and kept going. At last I felt the sand under my feet. I stood up and ran to the finish line. I felt numb and exhausted, as did everybody else.

I was happy with the amount of time it took me to swim the pier. During the rest of the summer, I improved each time we swam the pier. Swimming the pier was challenging, but each time I enjoyed it more as I improved. I impressed my friends with my amazing ability to swim the Huntington Pier.

Discussion:

1. What techniques did the author use to draw the reader into the story?

2. Did this story evoke any emotional response? If so, what was the response and how did the author evoke it?

3. Like the author, most of us have experienced challenging situations. On the back of this page, brainstorm experiences you have had that could be developed into an autobiographical incident.

Name:_____

Autobiographical Incident Frame

1. What was the main event?

_____

_____

_____

2. What was the setting?

_____

_____

_____

3. Sequence the events of your story. Brainstorm sensory details to include with each event.

Events	Sensory Details
1.	
2.	
3.	
4.	
5.	
6.	

4. How did the event conclude?

_____

_____

_____

Narrative Writing © 1998 Creative Teaching Press

Writer's Name: _____   Evaluator's Name: _____

Autobiographical Incident Rubric

	Great!	O.K.	Needs Help
Critical Components			
Written in first person			
Includes introduction and setting			
Describes details about the event in sequential order			
Includes a conclusion			
Style			
Word Choice Strong, active verbs			
Precise words			
Words that evoke images and express sensory detail			
Writing devices such as alliteration, metaphor, simile, onomatopoeia, and personification			
Coherence Clearly presented ideas			
Logically sequenced ideas			
Other Considerations			
Originality			
Characterization			
Dialogue			
Mechanics			
Ending punctuation			
Capitalization			
Comma rules			
Quotation marks			
Paragraph structure			

Narrative Writing © 1998 Creative Teaching Press

Ballad

Critical Components

A ballad is a story written in verse format. A ballad contains strong characters and vivid, dramatic action. A ballad is written in stanzas that have a strong rhythm but do not necessarily rhyme. A ballad often contains a two-line rhyming refrain that reflects an important element of the story. A ballad captures the emotion of the events as it tells the story.

Preparation

Bring to class several traditional ballads, such as "Casey at the Bat" or "Jesse James." (These can be found in anthologies, such as *As I Walked Out One Evening: A Book of Ballads* edited by Helen Plotz.) Make an overhead transparency of page 26. Photocopy pages 27 and 28 for students.

"CASEY AT THE BAT"

Setting the Stage

As a class, read aloud several ballads. Vary the oral reading method by inviting individuals or groups of students to read the verses, with the entire class joining in on the refrain.

Instructional Input

1. Make a chart or overhead transparency of the critical components of a ballad.

2. Examine the ballads read in class by comparing them to the list of critical components.

3. Ask students to comment on how well the ballads adhered to the components on the list. Record students' comments on the board.

Guided Practice

1. Display the overhead transparency of the student-authored ballads on page 26.

2. As a class, critique the ballads against the Ballad Rubric on page 28.

3. When students are comfortable with the critical components of a ballad, follow these procedures to develop a class ballad.

a) Select a historical event, a famous person, or a current school event as your topic.

Example:
The California Gold Rush

b) Brainstorm a list of the main events involved in the topic. Create a storyboard of these events. Each section of the storyboard will later be developed into a stanza of the ballad.

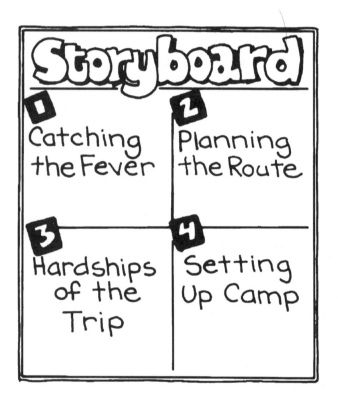

c) Compose a two-line rhyming refrain that reflects an important part of the story.

Example:
Get the pans and get the tools,
Hitch the wagons, load the mules

d) Decide on a stanza length (usually four lines) and a rhyming pattern. The stanzas do not need to rhyme, but once a pattern has been selected it should remain consistent throughout the ballad.

Example:
Stanza Length: 4 lines, 7–8 syllables per line
Rhyme Pattern: ABCB

We have the Golden Fever
We're off to the land of the sun
Hoping to make our fortune
Before our time on Earth is done

e) Work as a class to finish the ballad, or assign small groups of students to write specific stanzas.

Independent Practice

1. Invite students to work independently or in small groups, depending on ability level, to create their own ballads. Have them prewrite their ballads as they did as a group in step 3 of Guided Practice.

2. Provide students with the Ballad Frame on page 27 to assist them in following the procedures modeled in class. Also, give students the Ballad Rubric on page 28 to help them self-evaluate as they write.

Presentation

- Have students make posters depicting the character or events in the ballad. Post the ballads and the posters on a bulletin board or long school hallway titled *Room __'s Hall of Fame Ballads.*

- Distribute to the entire class copies of students' completed ballads. Each day, select one or two ballads for a choral presentation. Invite the author (or authors) of the ballad to read the stanzas while the whole class joins in the refrain.

Teaching Hints/Extensions

- Encourage students to dress as their ballad's main character or in the appropriate style of the historical time period and recite their ballads. (Invite them to include simple props as well.) Students may enjoy singing their ballad lyrics to an original or familiar tune. Invite parents or other classrooms to enjoy your students' creative presentations. Be sure to videotape the festivities.

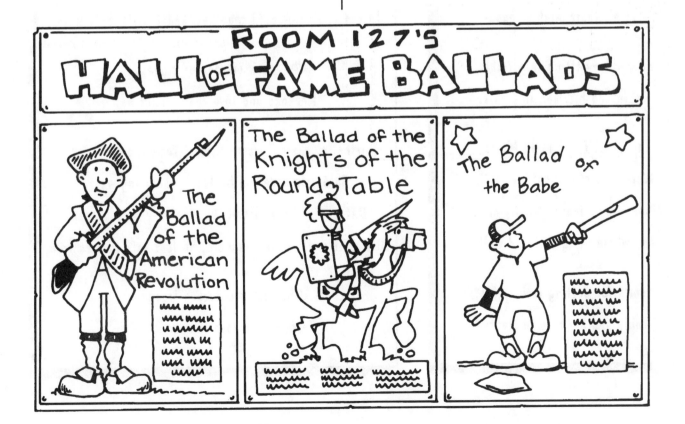

Ballad Samples

The Ballad of Robin Hood
Student Author: Matt Key

Robin Hood and Little John,
Friends until the end.
How are they to really know
What lies beyond the bend?

Known for getting into fights,
Robin and his men in tights.

"Rob the rich to feed the poor,"
Was the motto of their band.
The most beloved criminals
In all their mighty land.

Known for getting into fights,
Robin and his men in tights.

The Sheriff and Maid Marian
Were part of the tale we tell.
When King Richard finally came,
The whole thing finished well.

Known for getting into fights,
Robin and his men in tights.

The Ballad of Shakespeare's Plays
Student Author: Kelly Russell

"To be or not to be?" Hamlet questioned in this play.
"Revenge," said the ghost, "if I have my way."
Obedience to his king, to a father from his son,
But murder, such a sin, to ask out of love.

Oh, such murderous tragedy,
Revenge and love that cannot be.

Romeo and Juliet, a love that few will know.
Ones so sadly parted, for their families were foes.
Romeo was sent away from his Juliet.
In the end, they died together, and their people wept.

Oh, such murderous tragedy,
Revenge and love that cannot be.

Othello, a great warrior, most famous in his day,
So easily deceived by Iago's scheming ways.
Desdemona he so loved, but jealousy he'd choose.
And as it ends in Shakespeare, he lost this love so true.

Oh, such murderous tragedy,
Revenge and love that cannot be.

Narrative Writing © 1998 Creative Teaching Press

Ballad Frame

Directions:

1. Choose a topic.

2. Write a two-line rhyming refrain.

3. Create a storyboard of the events.

4. Decide on the rhyme scheme for the stanzas.

5. Write each stanza.

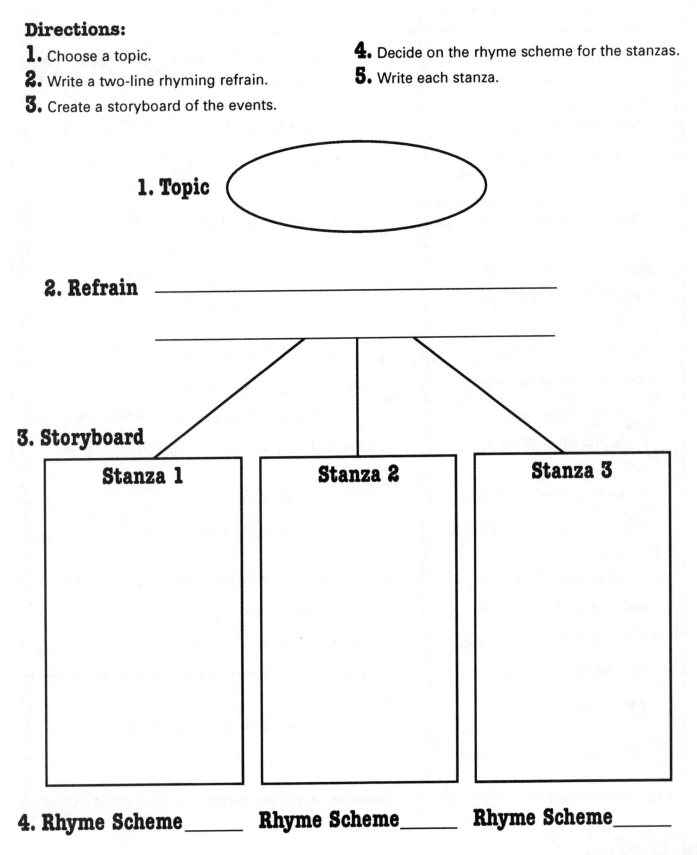

1. Topic

2. Refrain _____

_____

3. Storyboard

Stanza 1	Stanza 2	Stanza 3

4. Rhyme Scheme_____   **Rhyme Scheme**_____   **Rhyme Scheme**_____

Ballad Rubric

	Great!	O.K.	Needs Help
Critical Components			
Composed in verse format			
Contains strong characters			
Contains vivid dramatic action			
Includes stanzas with a strong, consistent rhythm			
Captures the emotion of the event(s)			
Style			
Word choice Strong, active verbs			
Precise words			
Words that evoke images and express sensory detail			
Writing devices such as alliteration, metaphor, simile, onomatopoeia, and personification			
Coherence Clearly presented ideas			
Logically sequenced ideas			
Originality			
Mechanics			
Ending punctuation			
Capitalization			
Comma rules			
Quotation marks			

Comments

_____

_____

_____

Narrative Writing © 1998 Creative Teaching Press

Biographical Sketch

Critical Components

A biographical sketch is a concise chrono-logical summary of a person's life written in third person. A biographical sketch tells about an individual's background, including his or her birth and death and family, friends, and interests. A biographical sketch describes a person's accomplishments, edu-cation, work, and contributions to society. A biographical sketch includes interesting anecdotes that reflect the person's character.

Preparation

Bring in books that include biographical sketches. Excellent examples include *Lives of the Writers, Lives of the Musicians,* and *Lives of the Artists* by Kathleen Krull and Kathryn Hewitt. Photocopy pages 32–34 for students.

Setting the Stage

Ask students to define *biography.* After elic-iting a definition, ask students to describe the difference between a painting and a sketch. Then, explain how a biography is like a painting because it includes a com-plete, detailed picture of a person's life. A biographical sketch, on the other hand, includes a quick look at only the most important aspects of a person's life, in the same way a sketch is quick and includes the most important parts of the picture.

Read an excerpt from one of Kathleen Krull and Kathryn Hewitt's books. (The sketch of E.B. White, author of *Charlotte's Web,* is highly recommended.) Discuss whether or not this biographical sketch is interesting and why. Ask students to be specific.

Instructional Input

1. Review with students the critical compo-nents of a biographical sketch. Challenge them to find those components in one of Krull and Hewitt's sketches or in the bio-graphical sketch on page 32.

2. After identifying the key components, write *personal information, accomplish-ments, anecdotes,* and *chronology* on the board. Then, challenge students to find examples of these elements in the same biographical sketch.

Guided Practice

1. Choose a student volunteer. Ask the following questions to interview the volunteer.

   Where were you born?

   Where have you gone to school?

   Tell us about your family.

   What have been your greatest accomplishments?

   What are your strongest attributes?

   Tell us an anecdote (humorous or serious) that reveals something about your character.

2. After interviewing the student, invite the class to retell the student's "story." Highlight major points on the board or overhead.

3. Sequence the events and, as a class, write a biographical sketch in third person.

Independent Practice

1. Invite students to work in pairs and interview one another, using the Biographical Sketch Frame on page 33.

2. After their interviews, have students write a biographical-sketch rough draft.

3. Once students have completed their rough drafts, encourage them to trade papers with their partners to ensure that the information is accurate.

4. Encourage students to continue comparing their manuscripts with the critical components listed on the Biographical Sketch Rubric (page 34) to ensure that the piece meets the appropriate criteria.

Presentation

- Compile final drafts in a classroom book titled *Room ___'s Biographical Sketches.* When a new student enrolls in your classroom, invite him or her to read this book. Encourage another member of the class to interview the new student and add the new student's biographical sketch to the class collection. Display this book at Back-to-School Night or Open House.

- Post biographical sketches on a bulletin board accompanied by photos of the students.

- Combine this project with an art project. Give each student two large pieces of brightly colored construction paper, glue, and scissors. Have students cut an outline of their head and torso from one large piece of construction paper and then create arms, legs, a head, a hat, and other attachments from the second piece of construction paper. Post their biographical sketch (authored by a classmate) on their torso and fold in the arms to hold the paper in place.

Teaching Hints/Extensions

- Invite students to interview family members and write individual biographical sketches to be kept in family records. Or, students can complete a long-term project that records a family history through a series of biographical sketches. These sketches can be compiled into a family album and accompanied by a family tree.

- Encourage students to research the lives of sports heroes, authors, musicians, and others in careers of interest. Divide the students into interest groups that write, illustrate, and publish their own theme-based biographical sketches in the same way as Kathleen Krull and Kathryn Hewitt did.

Biographical Sketch Sample

• Fred Nystrom •

Student Author: Tom Hoover

My great-great grandfather was Captain Fred Nystrom. He was born on the island of Gotland in Sweden in 1878. There he learned to be a fisherman. When he was 13, he signed up to sail on a merchant ship. He soon earned the position of second mate.

Later, he came to the U.S., where he enlisted in the Navy. After spending time in the Navy, he got his license to be captain of a sailing vessel at the age of 26, a very young age for a sea captain.

One memorable day, the captain and his wife, Elsa, sailed their ship into the San Francisco Bay. They arrived the day after the famous 1906 earthquake and fire had ravaged the city.

He returned to the sea and continued to have a good life, but he knew that times were changing and the new steam-powered boats would outdo the old sailing boats. So, he changed his career and became the third mate aboard a steamship. He moved his way up to captain once again. Altogether, he was the captain of 15 different steamships. He became known and respected all along the Pacific Coast.

In 1941, he became the Master of the ship *Admiral Y.S. Williams*. While in the Pacific, a typhoon left his ship stranded on the coast of Hong Kong. Little did he know that China was under invasion by the Japanese. Captain Nystrom became a prisoner of war in a terrible war camp in Hong Kong. He lost over 100 pounds and was constantly beaten. He was 64 years old, but still one of the strongest prisoners. He proved to be a leader among the other prisoners and many men said they would not have survived without him.

Even though he was 67 years old and had beriberi and tuberculosis and was starving, he would not go home at the end of the war until all of his crew was sent home first. He returned home to his family and died soon after at the age of 68. All who knew him remember his strength, character, and love of the sea.

Discussion:

1. Describe the accomplishments of Fred Nystrom.

2. How does the author describe his great-great grandfather's character?

Narrative Writing © 1998 Creative Teaching Press

Biographical Sketch Frame

Directions: Complete this page to begin prewriting a brief biographical sketch about a person of your choice. Your subject can be a family member, friend, or famous person.

Personal Information

Birth and Death (if applicable):_____

Family and Friends: _____

Interests and Hobbies: _____

_____

Personal Accomplishments

Education:_____

Work: _____

Contributions to Society: _____

_____

Personal Anecdotes

_____

_____

_____

_____

_____

_____

Biographical Sketch Rubric

	Great!	O.K.	Needs Help
Critical Components			
Written in third person			
Describes the subject's background			
Describes the subject's accomplishments			
Includes personal anecdotes			
Written in chronological order			
Style			
Word Choice Strong, active verbs			
Precise words			
Words that evoke images and express sensory detail			
Writing devices such as alliteration, metaphor, simile, onomatopoeia, and personification			
Coherence Clearly presented ideas			
Logically sequenced ideas			
Other Considerations			
Originality			
Characterization			
Dialogue			
Mechanics			
Ending punctuation			
Capitalization			
Comma rules			
Quotation marks			
Paragraph structure			

Narrative Writing © 1998 Creative Teaching Press

Short Story

Critical Components

A short story has an introduction that grabs the reader's attention, establishes the setting, and introduces the main character(s). A short story has an interesting conflict that heightens interest as the plot develops. A short story's conflict falls into one of three categories—character against character, character against himself or herself, or character against nature. A short story includes a single event, called the climax, at the peak of the interest level. A short story ends with a conclusion that follows the resolving of the conflict. This resolution often surprises the reader with a twist or "cliffhanger."

Preparation

Gather several short-story picture books of interest to your students. Make an overhead transparency of page 37. Photocopy pages 38–42 for students.

Setting the Stage

Read two or three short-story picture books that illustrate the critical components of a short story. Nearly any good picture book will work. *Grandfather's Journey* by Allen Say, *The Lorax* by Dr. Seuss, and *The Great Kapok Tree* by Lynne Cherry are high-interest stories with vivid illustrations. After reading each story, ask students the following questions and chart their responses on the board.

Did the author grab your attention at the beginning of the story? How?

Who were the character(s)?

What was the setting?

What was the main conflict in the story?

What was the climax?

How was the conflict resolved or was it resolved at all?

Instructional Input

1. Show students the overhead transparency of page 37. Discuss each component of the story plot. Refer back to the picture books to provide examples for each step.

2. Describe to students the three types of conflict encountered in stories—character against character, character against himself or herself, and character against nature. Discuss several familiar stories and identify in them the various types of conflict in story plots.

Guided Practice

1. Read aloud the two student-authored short stories on pages 38–40. As you read the stories, have students identify and evaluate the critical components of a short story's plot (introduction, setting, characters, rising action, conflict, climax, falling action, and conclusion).

2. As a class, brainstorm a random list of settings, conflicts, and characters for short stories. Write each item from the list on an index card, and place the cards in three baskets labeled *Setting, Conflict,* and *Characters.* Ask each student to draw a card from each basket and then write a spontaneous short story using the setting, conflict, and characters written on the cards. Encourage students to change any aspect of the story if they wish; however, this "basket draw" will help your reluctant writers get started. It will also generate some hilarious story lines.

Independent Practice

1. Show students the overhead of page 37 again. Briefly review each component of this Story Plot Mountain.

2. Have students jot down ideas about their own story plot, including specific notations on the various components of their story (introduction, rising action, climax, falling action, and conclusion). Invite students to use the Short Story Frame on page 41 to prewrite their story.

3. Set a timer for 30 minutes. (You may wish to vary the amount of time, depending on your students' ability level.) Ask students to begin a "quick write" rough draft of their short stories. Emphasize to students that they should not be concerned about spelling while writing the rough draft. Students often come up with powerful

and creative stories when they do not have to focus on mechanics.

4. Once rough drafts have been written, invite students to use the Short Story Rubric on page 42 to critique and rewrite their own papers. After they have polished their early drafts, encourage peer and teacher critiquing using the same rubric. Allow time for students to make revisions before final publishing.

Presentation

- Require students to type and illustrate their final drafts. Let them know that having a classmate illustrate their story is perfectly acceptable so long as they give him or her credit as the illustrator. Encourage self-publishing of illustrated short stories using binders and laminated covers.

Teaching Hints/Extensions

- Enthusiastic students often want to write multiple-chapter books. Encourage this, but introduce some structure to the process. Explain to students that writing a novel with many chapters can be similar to writing several related short stories. Each chapter has a "mini-plot" that contributes to the larger plot. The difference is that each chapter may end with a cliffhanger, and the final resolution of the overarching conflict is saved for the end of the book. Before beginning novel writing, invite students to create one-chapter sequels to their original short stories.

Story Plot Mountain

Short Story
Sample 1

• Aliens •

Student Author: Trenton Dyck

Have you ever been abducted by an alien? I have. I was at the playground one beautiful morning when all of a sudden it was covered by a looming shadow. The shadow became bigger and bigger and bigger. When I turned around, I saw an alien spaceship that was fluorescent blue with a green ring around it.

Then a six-eyed Martian about two feet tall held my squirming body and zapped me into the spaceship. The inside of the spaceship was many different colors. It was not like any color you have ever seen. The green aliens could write but could not talk.

They decided they were going to do an experiment on me. They tied me up with green goo that I could not get out of! They pushed a red button. I then realized I had become two feet tall, green, and six-eyed. Then, all the Martians remembered that tampering with human beings makes them dissolve. So they dissolved. I found that I had to drive the spaceship. It was actually pretty easy, except for navigating through an asteroid belt.

I landed on Earth. I went to a hot dog store and everyone screamed and ran out the doorway. Somebody left their juicy hot dog behind and I ate it.

All of a sudden I became a human again. I ran home puffing as fast as I could. I told my mom why I had been late. She did not believe me one bit.

Short Story
Sample 2

• Small Is Good •

Student Author: Matthew Thompson

"No! I don't want him. You take him."

"I had him last time. It's your turn. Besides, if you take him we'll be 'It' first."

"No way!"

I hid in a corner listening to them arguing over whose team I was going to have to be on. For as long as I could remember, I've been a weak, puny salmon—nothing like my other salmon friends. For the eight years I've lived in this creek and the four years I lived in the ocean, I was always smaller than everyone else. I used to think that being small was a disadvantage. I was always being pushed around by everyone. I always had to watch for some other bully fish. Also, every time we picked teams for a game of Salmon, I was picked last, even though I was very good at squeezing into cracks to hide. (So you know, the game Salmon is similar to the game Sardines).

It wasn't until we all headed upstream to go home that I realized being small wasn't so bad. We had traveled for four weeks, 98 miles from the San Francisco Bay up the Sacramento River. We had 70 miles to go before we reached Battle Creek. It had been tough swimming upstream and over waterfalls and dams, but it was easier for me since I was smaller and lighter and could jump higher and farther than anyone else.

We had just left Lake Shasta. I was pretty sore from climbing up the lake's dam. Right then, I noticed we were missing some of the females from our group. I called to our salmon leader, "Salmon Leader! Some of the females are missing!"

"How many? When did you realize this?" he replied.

"About four, and I noticed right after we left the lake."

"Where did you last see them?" he asked.

I replied, "I saw them when we went up the ladder at the dam."

The salmon leader paused and then turned to a messenger and said in a stern voice, "Hurry and go tell the scout fish to stop the group and rest until we return."

"Yes, sir!" he said and hurried off. The leader turned to me and said, "Let's go!"

We went back to the lake. "You go this way and I'll go the other way. Meet me back here in five minutes," he said.

I took off, calling their names as I swam, "Mrs. Salmon!" Nobody answered. I thought, "Why would they wander away from the group? Did they want to lay their eggs?" I looked around. There was a lot of food, but I wasn't hungry. Then, out of the corner of my eye, I spotted some eggs that must have floated away from the nest. "Maybe they belong to the missing females," I thought. I went to retrieve them.

As I grabbed them, I felt a sharp pain. The pain startled me and I tried to swim away. Something pulled me. I fought for awhile, but I grew tired. Then I saw a huge, black, floating rock, and I was headed right for it! I was pulled to the surface and a green net came around me and lifted me out of the water. I wiggled around trying to get back into the water. I heard deep voices and saw two men looking at me. I remembered how one old salmon had said something about people and how they cut you open and eat you. As they looked at me, one said, "He's just a little guy. I say we throw him back. What do you think he is, a couple pounds?"

The other man said, "I agree. Quit wiggling, little guy. I almost got it . . . there!"

"There he goes! Ha! He didn't want to stick around."

I swam away as fast as I could. I was bleeding in my mouth, but I didn't care. I found a safe spot and rested for awhile. Then I met up with the leader and we went back to the group. Salmon Leader had had more luck. He found two of the females. I feared the worst for the other two.

I realized later that it was my size that saved my life. Other salmon may tease me, but there are always some advantages to being small. So, if friends are teasing you because you're different, just remember this story.

Oh! When we made it home, I won the highest-jump award.

Narrative Writing © 1998 Creative Teaching Press

Name:_____

Short Story Frame

Directions: Fill in the following information before writing your short story.

1. Describe the **setting.** _____

_____

_____

2. Describe the **character(s).**_____

_____

_____

3. Describe the main **conflict.** _____

_____

_____

4. What **obstacle(s)** will the character need to overcome in order to solve the problem?

_____

_____

_____

5. How will the character(s) overcome the obstacles and bring **resolution** to the problem?

_____

_____

_____

Writer's Name: _____   Evaluator's Name: _____

Short Story Rubric

	Great!	O.K.	Needs Help
Critical Components			
Includes a strong beginning that grabs the reader's attention			
Establishes the setting during the introduction			
Introduces the major character(s) during the introduction			
Includes an interesting conflict (character against character, character against himself or herself, or character against nature)			
Includes a climax			
Conclusion follows a resolution, surprise, or "cliffhanger"			
Style			
Word choice			
Strong, active verbs			
Precise words			
Words that evoke images and express sensory detail			
Writing devices such as alliteration, metaphor, simile, onomatopoeia, and personification			
Coherence			
Clearly presented ideas			
Logically sequenced ideas			
Other Considerations			
Originality			
Characterization			
Dialogue			
Mechanics			
Ending punctuation			
Capitalization			
Comma rules			
Quotation marks			
Paragraph structure			

Narrative Writing © 1998 Creative Teaching Press

Fable

Critical Components

A fable is a brief, fanciful tale. A fable's characters often include animals that talk and act like people (personification). A fable has an introduction, a problem, and an outcome. A fable's problem is related to the weakness of a character or characters. A fable teaches a lesson about life. A fable ends with a moral that summarizes the lesson.

Preparation

Bring to class several fable anthologies, such as Arnold Lobel's *Fables* or *Demi's Reflective Fables* by Demi. Photocopy pages 46–49 for students.

Setting the Stage

Write several well-known proverbs on the board, such as *Pride goeth before a fall, Look before you leap, He who laughs last laughs best, Everything comes to those who wait, Don't put the carriage before the horse, Haste makes waste,* and *Don't count your chickens before they hatch.* Discuss the meaning of each of these proverbs and others with which students are familiar. Tell students that a key component of fables is the incorporation of lessons or morals. The lesson or moral is illustrated through the fable's story and succinctly summarized at the end of the fable in the form of a proverb.

Provide a brief historical background of fables. Some of the first fables were told more than 3,000 years ago by a Greek slave named Aesop. Because of his position as a slave, he could not directly preach or lecture to people. Instead, he embedded his lessons in engaging, nonthreatening stories about animals who displayed the weaknesses of human beings. Some of Aesop's fables are still popular today. Share with students one of these familiar fables, such as "The Tortoise and the Hare."

Instructional Input

1. Distribute copies of the student-authored fable on page 46 and read it aloud with your class. Also read aloud several fables from an anthology such as Arnold Lobel's *Fables* or *Demi's Reflective Fables*. Ask students what each of these fables has in common.

2. Review the critical components of fables. Make a chart on the board that includes the following categories: *fable title, animal characters, human characteristics, problem, resolution,* and *moral.* As each category is discussed, record the appropriate information for each of the fables.

3. Introduce the term *personification,* an important element in fables. Reread several fables and ask students to determine the human characteristics of each animal character. (For instance, in "The Tortoise and the Hare", the primary human characteristic of the hare is overconfidence. The primary trait of the tortoise is determination.)

4. Record the animals and their primary characteristics on the chart. Explain that because a fable must be written simply, each animal character is usually associated with one primary human-like character trait.

5. Remind students that because a fable is a type of short story, it will include an introduction, a conflict, and a resolution (conclusion). Discuss the conflict, resolution, and correlating moral that occurs in each of the fables you have read. Record responses on the chart.

Guided Practice

1. Distribute a copy of the student-authored fable on page 47 to each student.

2. Have students read the fable and answer the accompanying questions.

3. Upon completion, allow time for a discussion that highlights the importance of simplicity, originality, and the direct correlation of the characters' actions and the lesson learned (the moral).

Fable Title	Animal Characters	Human Characteristics	Problem	Resolution	Moral
The Tortoise and the Hare	Tortoise	determination	too slow	wins	Slow and steady wins the race.
	Hare	overconfidence	too cocky	loses	

Independent Practice

1. Provide each student with a copy of the Fable Frame on page 48.

2. Have students use the frame to develop their own fable rough draft.

3. Invite students to edit each other's work and revise their own to create a publishable final draft.

Presentation

- Invite each student to read aloud his or her fable to a small group, omitting the moral. Challenge the author's classmates to each write an appropriate moral to the story and share it with the author. If classmates' written morals differ, discuss how writing the fable more simply and directly will lead to a common conclusion. After this group input, allow time for students to edit and revise their fable as necessary.

- Since fables have a long oral tradition, encourage students to share their final fables in a creative oral presentation, such as an audiotaped version with sound effects; a puppet show using stick, paper bag, or finger puppets; or an "Ancient Aesop" television show using videotape or live performance.

Teaching Tips/Extensions

- After students have written an initial fable, you may wish to extend this lesson by having students work with a partner to create an additional "tangram fable."

- Read aloud *Grandfather Tang's Story* by Ann Tompert. In this book, Grandfather uses tangram shapes to illustrate the animals in the story he is telling his granddaughter. The story incorporates the critical components of a fable and ends with a moral. As you read, demonstrate with tangram pieces on the overhead projector each of the animal characters Grandfather mentions. After sharing the story, provide each pair of students with two sets of the seven tangram pieces. (Pieces can be cut from construction paper.) Invite students to use these pieces to create two animal character shapes using all seven pieces for each animal and to develop a fable around these characters. Have students share their fables with the class by having one partner read the fable while the other partner positions the tangram pieces on the overhead projector.

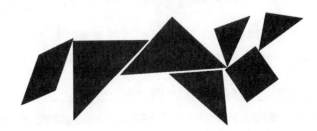

Fable
Sample 1

• The Snake and the Lizard •

Student Author: Michelle Encarnacion

Snake and Lizard had a fight one day. Snake boasted about how easily he could shed his skin. Lizard boasted about how effortlessly he could pluck off his tail.

"I bet you can't get a single piece of skin off you," sneered Snake.

"Well, I'd like to see you break off your tail," retorted Lizard.

"We'll just have to have a contest then, won't we?" challenged Snake.

"Fine," Lizard answered.

So both animals positioned themselves for the contest. Lizard tried to show off by doing a few push-ups . . . but after not being able to get back up after the first push-up, he decided to just hook a piece of his skin onto the thorn of a bush and wait for the snake to be ready. The hooking part hurt a little . . . well, it hurt a lot. But either way, Lizard was too competitive to notice.

Snake was also trying to warm up for the contest. He thought he'd show off to his rival by doing some push-ups, since the lizard obviously couldn't do any. But he remembered he had no arms, so he decided to just wrap his tail around a large rock and psyche himself up for the contest.

"Ready, set, GO!" Lizard screamed.

Snake slithered away from the rock as quickly as he could while Lizard ran from the bush as fast as his scrawny little legs could scramble.

Then, to their surprise, Snake saw he had succeeded in removing his tail. Unfortunately, all that was left of him was his head. (Everyone knows that a snake's body is all tail!) The snake was extremely embarrassed. He called out to Lizard because he could not see him. Lizard came out from behind some grass, pink as an eraser. His skin was completely gone! Lizard was not hurt in any way, but he felt rather cold.

Both animals did not say a word. All they could do was look at each other with wide-open mouths.

Moral: *Pride profits no one.*

Narrative Writing © 1998 Creative Teaching Press

Fable
Sample 2

• Got Milk? •

Student Author: Brooke Christensen

It was a beautiful day, not a cloud in sight. It was also Cow's birthday and Rabbit was throwing a surprise party for her. Rabbit had been working hard. In fact, she'd been up all night getting ready. Now, all that was left to do was to bake the cake.

As Rabbit gathered her ingredients, she realized she had no milk. "Oh what shall I do! With no milk, I can't make a cake and with no cake, there can't be a party! Oh dear, dear me, whatever shall I do?"

As Rabbit grew more distressed, she thought, "If there's no party, none of our friends will come. In fact, we'll probably lose all our friends." "Oh," she moaned, "the blame will come straight to me. Oh dear, dear me, whatever shall I do?" Rabbit got herself in such a depressed state that she got a headache and went to bed, sure she would die.

Shortly thereafter came a knock on the door. The noise roused Rabbit. "Come in," she groaned.

Cow stepped through the door. "Rabbit," she called, "I gave a little extra milk today. If you could take some off my hands, I would be grateful."

Moral: *On a sunny day, if you look for storm clouds, it may rain.*

Discussion:

1. Who is the main character in this fable?

2. How does personification let the reader know more about the characters?

3. What human characteristics does each character demonstrate?

4. What problem is encountered?

5. How is this problem resolved?

6. Do you think the moral is a logical lesson to be learned from this story? Why or why not?

Name:_____

Fable Frame

1. Describe the lesson or **moral** you would like your characters to learn.
(Note: When you write your fable, the moral will appear at the end, but you need to decide on your moral first so your characters' actions will lead to the moral.)

_____

_____

2. Describe the **problem** the characters will encounter.

_____

_____

3. Describe the **resolution** of the problem.

_____

_____

4. Describe your **setting**.

_____

_____

5. Describe your **characters**.

Character one: _____

Human characteristic: _____

Character two: _____

Human characteristic: _____

*Try to show the reader your characters' major traits through their words and actions.
**Be sure to make the characters' actions lead to the resolution, which will illustrate the lesson or moral.

Narrative Writing © 1998 Creative Teaching Press

Writer's Name: _____   Evaluator's Name: _____

Fable Rubric

	Great!	O.K.	Needs Help
Critical Components			
Brief and fanciful			
Includes animal characters that talk and act like people			
Contains an introduction, a problem, and a resolution			
Contains a problem related to the weakness of a character or characters			
Teaches a lesson about life			
Ends with a moral that summarizes the lesson			
Style			
Word Choice Strong, active verbs			
Precise words			
Words that evoke images and express sensory detail			
Writing devices such as alliteration, metaphor, simile, onomatopoeia, and personification			
Coherence Clearly presented ideas			
Logically sequenced ideas			
Other Considerations			
Originality			
Characterization			
Dialogue			
Mechanics			
Ending punctuation			
Capitalization			
Comma rules			
Quotation marks			
Paragraph structure			

Fairy Tale

Critical Components

A fairy tale is a short story that involves love and/or adventure. The first sentence of the story identifies it as a fairy tale. Typical examples include *Once upon a time* and *Long ago, when wishes still came true.* A fairy tale includes a magical event as a key element in the story. A fairy tale includes a hero or heroine and a villain. A fairy tale's characters often include royalty and animals. A fairy tale ends happily, often closing with *They lived happily ever after.*

Preparation

Bring to class one traditional fairy tale, such as *Snow White* or *Jack and the Beanstalk* and an alternative version of the same tale, such as *Snow White in New York* by Fiona French or *Jack and the Meanstalk* by Brian and Rebecca Wildsmith. If you have difficulty locating a modernized fairy tale, photocopy the student-authored sample on pages 53 and 54. Photocopy pages 55 and 56 for students.

Setting the Stage

Read a traditional fairy tale to the class. Ask students what changes they would make to update or modernize this tale. Ask them to name modern inventions, activities, or daily life experiences that could be incorporated into the story. Allow time for discussion and record student responses on the board. Next, share the modernized version of the traditional tale and discuss similarities and differences between it and the ideas your class discussed. Finally, read aloud the student-authored fairy tale *Rapunzel and the Bad Hair Day* (pages 53 and 54). Discuss ways the author's updates add humor to the classic fairy tale.

Instructional Input

1. Elicit from students elements that most fairy tales have in common. Chart responses on the board. Refer to the Critical Components section of this lesson and add any missing elements to the chart.

Fairy Tale Elements:

• Usually starts with "Once upon a time...."
• Involves magic.
• Usually has a hero and a villian.
• Often has a "royal" character.
• Animals can be important characters.
• Ends happily.

2. Tell the class that even when a fairy tale is modernized, these elements will still be present. Have the class choose a traditional fairy tale and brainstorm and list on the board possible changes and modernizations. For example, Cinderella could meet Prince Charming at a long-distance race. Instead of arriving in a horse-drawn carriage, she could arrive at the race on a freshly detailed motorcycle. Instead of a glass slipper, she could leave behind a basketball sneaker.

Guided Practice

1. Distribute and reread as a class the Fairy Tale Sample from pages 53 and 54.

2. Have students circle in this sample all traditional fairy tale elements in blue and underline all modernizations in red.

Independent Practice

1. Provide students with the Fairy Tale Frame on page 55 to assist them in developing their own modernized fairy tale.

2. Have students complete the frame as the prewriting stage of the writing process.

3. Have students write rough drafts, revise, and edit until they have created publishable work.

Presentation

- Publish a class *Fairy Tale Anthology,* complete with illustrations and information about each author. Group together tales with similar characters or morals. Make copies for the library and school office.

- Invite students to create a salt-dough relief map depicting the setting of their fairy tale. Students should be encouraged to include all mentioned elements, such as a castle or an enchanted forest. Mount the fairy tales on construction paper and display them on a wall above the relief maps. Check with a local library or museum. Many are eager to display local student work.

Salt Dough

Ingredients:

2 cups (500 ml) flour
1/2 cup (125 ml) salt
2 tsp. (10 ml) cream of tartar
1 cup (250 ml) water
food coloring (optional)

Directions: Mix ingredients. Knead. Keep in an airtight container until ready to use. Makes enough dough for one to two small relief maps.

Teaching Hints/Extensions

- Invite students to rewrite fairy tales from the perspectives of specific characters. For example, students may rewrite the story of Snow White from the perspective of Prince Charming or the Wicked Queen. Read aloud books such as *The True Story of the Three Little Pigs* by Jon Scieszka before beginning this assignment.

- Frequently, different cultures have versions of the same fairy tale as part of their folklore. Read aloud several multicultural versions of the same story. For example, you might share *Yeh-Shen* by Ai-Ling Louie, *The Brocaded Slipper* by Lynette Dyer Vuong, and *Mufaro's Beautiful Daughters* by John Steptoe. (These are Chinese, Vietnamese, and African versions of *Cinderella.*) Compare and contrast similarities among and differences between the stories. Ask students to speculate how and why these same stories appear in different cultures.

Fairy Tale Sample

• Rapunzel and the Bad Hair Day •

Student Author: Gabriel Encarnacion

Once upon a time, not too long ago, there lived a girl named Rapunzel. She resided in a beautiful high-rise building in New York City. She had all the things that any girl could possibly want, but still she was unhappy. You see, her father, a rich executive, refused to have her hair cut by just any person in New York. Her hairdresser had to be the best. So, he would go off to faraway lands in search of the perfect hairdresser.

One time, he returned to find that his daughter's hair was growing longer and longer, but he just ignored it and said that he would someday find the perfect hairdresser for his sweet little girl. After one of his expeditions, however, he returned to his front door to find a stream of long, blonde hair. He was quite alarmed and rushed to his daughter's room, which was on the third floor. There, he saw his daughter surrounded by her fifty foot long hair! "My dear Rapunzel! How did this happen?" he asked. "Well," she began, "I haven't had my hair cut for the longest time and now it has become like this!"

Her father was worried. If the news got out that his daughter had the longest hair in the world, his career would be ruined. He would be the laughingstock of New York. So, he devised a plan. He would lock Rapunzel in her room until he could finally find the perfect person to cut her hair. "I'm only doing this for your good," he said to his daughter. But his assurances were drowned out by Rapunzel's sobbing. He rushed out of the room and locked the door. Of course, he was not totally cruel—he still let the maids bring her food and water, but aside from that, no human contact was allowed.

One day, Prince Charming was selling bottled water in the neighborhood and saw a wave of long hair sweeping out of the window of a house. Curious, he stepped up to the hair and pulled on it. A scream erupted from the window, startling Prince Charming. A beautiful girl stuck her head out from the window and asked, "Who pulled on my hair?"

Prince Charming was amazed! This was the girl that belonged to the long hair. "Why don't you come down? I'd like to sell you some bottled water!"

"I can't!" said Rapunzel in dismay. "My father has locked me up in this room because he is worried that people might get ideas about my long hair."

"What kind of ideas?" asked Prince Charming.

"They might think that I'm a freak, and that would ruin his career," Rapunzel said as she broke into tears.

Narrative Writing © 1998 Creative Teaching Press

Prince Charming felt sorry for the dear girl and decided to help her out. "Miss," he said, for he still did not know her name, "I'd be more than willing to help you out of your room. Just hold on to your hair!"

Before Rapunzel could ask why she had to hold on, she let out a terrifying scream. She looked out the window and there was Prince Charming, climbing to her room using her hair! "AAAAAAAAAA!!! WHAT ARE YOU DOING?! IT'S COMING OUT BY THE ROOTS!!" screamed Rapunzel.

Although it wasn't coming out by the roots, the hair was tearing off in long strands, making it quite hard for Prince Charming to climb up. Finally, he made it and climbed into the room. There stood Rapunzel, except her hair was now shoulder-length!

"It looks beautiful," she explained. "Thank you so much Mr. . . . ah . . . uh . . ."

"Charming," piped in the man. "I am Prince Charming."

"Oh my!" said Rapunzel. "Royalty! Well, pardon my manners, Your Highness, but I was not aware that . . ."

"No, actually my first name is Prince and my last name is Charming. But please, call me Mr. Charming."

"My name is Rapunzel," she said.

"What does 'Rapunzel' mean?" asked Mr. Charming.

"'She Who Screams at the Top of Her Lungs'," the girl replied.

Just as Rapunzel was about to hug Mr. Charming, her father burst in the door screaming, "Rapunzel! Rapunzel! I found the perfect hairdresser for you! He lives in Europe and I'll take you there right awa . . . WHAT IS HE DOING IN MY DAUGHTER'S ROOM??!!" He was fuming when he saw Prince Charming. "I'd like to let you know, young man, that I have a very extensive gun collection!" But before he could spurt out any more threats, Rapunzel told him how Prince Charming had tried to save her and, in the process, had cut her hair to a manageable length. Her father loved the new haircut and said he was sorry for his irrational behavior. He also thanked Prince Charming for his services and invited him to stay for dinner.

In the end, everyone was happy. Rapunzel's father didn't have to spend all that money on a European hairdresser and there was no threat to his career. Prince Charming received an order for a year's supply of bottled water from Rapunzel, and Rapunzel would see Mr. Charming each month so he could climb her hair to make it just the right length.

Narrative Writing © 1998 Creative Teaching Press

Fairy Tale Frame

1. Select a familiar fairy tale.

_____

2. List the traditional elements of the fairy tale. Then list modernizations of these elements you can include in an updated version to add interest and entertainment.

Traditional Elements	Modernizations

3. Complete the chart below, providing information about the original fairy tale as well as about your new updated version.

Original Fairy Tale		Modernized Version
Characters		
Setting		
Magical Elements		
Problem		
Solution		

Fairy Tale Rubric

	Great!	O.K.	Needs Help
Critical Components			
Involves love and/or adventure			
Includes "Fairy Tale" opening			
Includes a magical event as a key element in the story			
Includes a hero or heroine and a villain			
Includes royalty and/or animal characters			
Ends happily			
Style			
Word choice Strong, active verbs			
Precise words			
Words that evoke images and express sensory detail			
Writing devices such as alliteration, metaphor, simile, onomatopoeia, and personification			
Coherence Clearly presented ideas			
Logically sequenced ideas			
Other Considerations			
Originality			
Characterization			
Dialogue			
Mechanics			
Ending punctuation			
Capitalization			
Comma rules			
Quotation marks			
Paragraph structure			

Narrative Writing © 1998 Creative Teaching Press

Tall Tale

Critical Components

A tall tale is a short story that features a "larger-than-life" character with unusual skills or abilities. These abilities are often described through simile and metaphor. The conflict resolution in a tall tale involves the character's unusual skills or abilities. A tall tale uses extreme exaggeration *(hyperbole)*. Tall tales are usually humorous. They are written in a matter-of-fact "deadpan" style that adds to the humor.

Preparation

Bring to class illustrated tall tales, such as the books written by Steven Kellogg featuring Johnny Appleseed, Paul Bunyan, Pecos Bill, and Mike Fink. Make an overhead transparency of page 60. Photocopy pages 61–63 for students.

Setting the Stage

Divide the class into small groups. Give each group a different illustrated tall tale, a copy of the Tall Tale Frame (page 62), and a piece of poster board or butcher paper. Invite the groups to read their tall tales and record on the frame the appropriate information from the story. Invite students to use this information to design a poster or humorous illustration of their character, stressing the character's special skills and abilities. Allow time for groups to share their posters with the class. Display all completed posters on a tall tale bulletin board.

Instructional Input

1. Ask the class what each of the tall tales had in common. (They all included the same critical components.) Record student responses on the chalkboard and discuss each component.

2. Define the term *hyperbole* by emphasizing the difference between it and exaggeration. (A hyperbole is such an extreme exaggeration that it is not to be taken literally. For example, the statement *I'm so hungry I could eat a horse* is a hyperbole. The statement *I'm so hungry I could eat five hamburgers* is an exaggeration, but may be within the realm of possibility.) Also explain how deadpan humor does not draw attention to funny situations. Instead, it treats all situations, no matter how ridiculous, with the same serious tone.

3. Ask students to speculate how and where tall tales originated. (Tall tales originated in North America. Early settlers from Europe were faced with the hardships of settling a vast, wild country with overwhelming natural resources and severe weather. Tall tales reflect these hardships and the pride Americans had in the strength, courage, and cleverness of these early settlers.)

4. Discuss how tall tales are a type of short story and follow the same basic framework as short stories, including an introduction, a conflict, and a resolution to the conflict. The conflict and resolution are related to the main characters' unique abilities.

5. Review the concepts of metaphor and simile with students (see pages 10 and 11). Explain how these writing devices are frequently used in tall tales. Invite students to locate examples of simile and metaphor in the tall tales they read earlier.

Guided Practice

1. Display the overhead transparency of page 60. Read and enjoy this student-authored tall tale with your class.

2. As a class, brainstorm similes and/or metaphors that could be added to this story to further enhance its effectiveness. For example, *Tom's ears were as big as cantaloupes sprouting from the side of his head.*

3. Distribute to students copies of page 61. Discuss with students how the author introduced the story, provided examples of Sam's unique ability (using hyperbole, exaggeration, metaphor, and simile), and used Sam's unique ability to solve the problem.

"Big Mouth Sam"

4. Ask students to underline all examples of hyperbole and exaggeration, marking hyperbole with an *H* and exaggeration with an *E*. Ask them to circle similes and metaphors.

5. Conclude the assignment by discussing with students the topics at the bottom of the page.

6. Brainstorm with students original tall tale characters and their amazing abilities. Record responses on the board.

Independent Practice

1. Provide each student with a copy of the Tall Tale Frame on page 62.

2. Have each student develop an original tall tale character and complete the frame. Invite students to use the frame to assist them in writing rough drafts of their tall tales.

Presentation

- Invite students to copy their tall tale onto a "tall" butcher-paper figure of their hero/heroine. Encourage students to include as many appropriate physical characteristics as possible (for example, bulging muscles or huge ears). If you run out of display space in your classroom, these tall heroes can be posted in school hallways, the cafeteria, or the office.

Teaching Hints/Extensions

- If students experience difficulty choosing a tall tale hero/heroine, ask them to think of current problems our society faces. Invite them to brainstorm friends, sports heroes, politicians, or movie stars and how one of these individuals might contribute to solving one of these problems. Challenge students to use exaggeration and turn one of these people into a larger-than-life tall tale hero.

- Encourage students to brainstorm the downside of fame. What problems might their character encounter because of his or her unique appearance or abilities? Invite students to compete in a "So You Think You Have Troubles?" contest in which they write and present a brief, humorous monologue written from their character's perspective.

Tall Tale
Sample 1

• **Tom Big Ears** •

Student Author: Katrina Hare

Tom Big Ears, as everyone called him, was an average-sized man, but he had ears that were so big that they rested on his shoulders. He was also something of a genius. Just a week after he was born, Tom could talk to his parents, read novels, and hear everything within a mile of wherever he was.

I came to know Tom when he moved next door to me. He was really nice, but everyone thought that he was strange. After awhile though, he won people's love. Tom saved a cow from getting run over by a train, because he heard the train coming from a mile away. He saved a child from drowning, because he heard the boy screaming underneath the water at the pool. Tom performed many heroic feats. But the rich, handsome mayor did not like Tom because everyone in the city loved Tom more than him.

One day, Tom overheard a plan to rob the city treasury. Tom notified the police and had the robbers arrested. The mayor was so happy that he gave Tom an award for helping his city. No one ever made fun of Tom's gigantic ears again—not even the mayor.

Narrative Writing © 1998 Creative Teaching Press

Tall Tale
Sample 2

• Big Mouth Sam •

Student Author: David Stough

A long, long time ago, in a small town in Mississippi, a baby boy was born to a very happy mother and father. They named him Sam. For his first year, Sam seemed normal enough, but as time went on, his mom and dad began to notice some strange things that weren't so normal. For instance, any time Sam drank water, he liked to hold the water in his mouth for five minutes before he swallowed it. His mother always said he was like a chipmunk with too much food in his mouth. And whenever he swam in a lake or a pond, his parents also noticed that he would try to suck up as much of the lake as he could, and the lake always seemed smaller when they left.

One day Sam's mother went outside to milk the cow and stood in shock as she witnessed her five-year-old son with half of their pond in his mouth. Sam's cheeks had stretched out at least two feet. She ran back in the house to get her husband, who was equally amazed. The older Sam got, the more water he could store in his mouth. His mouth was a huge dam holding immense amounts of water.

One morning, as Sam was walking through the forest, he saw billows of smoke atop a nearby tree. Sam ran to investigate. As he got closer, he saw huge flames engulfing a small cabin and most of the surrounding woods. Sam knew that he had to act fast, so he quickly ran to the closest water source he could find, which happened to be the Mississippi River. With a deep breath, he sucked up more than half of the entire river! This time his cheeks had stretched to be as enormous as mountains! He ran as fast as he could back to the fire and opened his mouth. Immediately, the water came out like the sound of thunder and the flames were quickly put out. The cabin, on the other hand, floated about two miles downstream before settling on dry land. A frightened and wet family slowly came out of the house and thanked Sam for his bravery. Some say that Sam still walks around the state of Mississippi helping people in any way that he can using his strange and amazing ability.

Discussion:

1. What was Sam's unique ability?

2. What examples did the author give to illustrate this ability?

3. What problem did Sam encounter?

4. How did Sam use his special abilities to solve the problem?

Name:_____

Tall Tale Frame

Directions: Name your character and describe the setting, conflict, and resolution. List two or more major accomplishments. Underneath the accomplishment, write examples of exaggerations and hyperboles to illustrate the accomplishments.

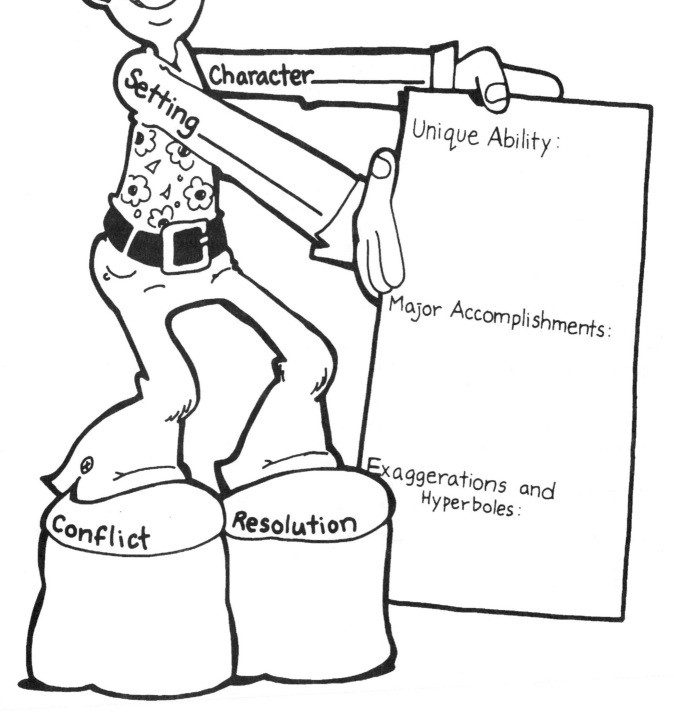

Setting

Character_____

Unique Ability:

Major Accomplishments:

Exaggerations and Hyperboles:

Conflict   Resolution

Narrative Writing © 1998 Creative Teaching Press

Writer's Name: _____   Evaluator's Name: _____

Tall Tale Rubric

	Great!	O.K.	Needs Help
Critical Components			
Introduces a larger-than-life character at the beginning			
Includes exaggeration and hyperbole			
Includes simile and metaphor			
Written in "deadpan" style			
Conflict resolution involves the special skills and/or abilities of the main character			
Style			
Word choice Strong, active verbs			
Precise words			
Words that evoke images and express sensory detail			
Writing devices such as alliteration, metaphor, simile, onomatopoeia, and personification			
Coherence Clearly presented ideas			
Logically sequenced ideas			
Other Considerations			
Originality			
Characterization			
Dialogue			
Mechanics			
Ending punctuation			
Capitalization			
Comma rules			
Quotation marks			
Paragraph structure			

Bibliography

Professional Resource Books

Batzle, Janine. *Portfolio Assessment and Evaluation.* Creative Teaching Press, 1992.

Elbow, Peter. *Writing with Power: Techniques for Mastering the Writing Process.* Oxford, 1981.

Flynn, Kris. *Graphic Organizers.* Creative Teaching Press, 1995.

Graves, Donald H. *A Fresh Look at Writing.* Heinemann, 1994.

McCarthy, Tara. 150 *Thematic Writing Activities.* Scholastic, 1993.

Miller, Wilma H. *Alternative Assessment Techniques for Reading & Writing.* Center for Applied Research in Education, 1995.

Schifferle, Judith. *Editorial Skills.* Center for Applied Research in Education, 1985.

Schifferle, Judith. *Word Skills.* Center for Applied Research in Education, 1985.

Sparks, J.E. *Write for Power.* Communication Associates, 1995.

Sunflower, Cherlyn. *Really Writing! Ready-to-Use Writing Process Activities for the Elementary Grades.* Center for Applied Research in Education, 1994.

Ballads

Plotz, Helen (editor). *As I Walked Out One Evening: A Book of Ballads.* Morrow, 1976.

Thayer, Ernest Lawrence. *Casey at the Bat.* Atheneum, 1995.

Biographical Sketches

Krull, Kathleen and Kathryn Hewitt. *Lives of the Artists.* Harcourt Brace Jovanovich, 1992.

Krull, Kathleen and Kathryn Hewitt. *Lives of the Musicians.* Harcourt Brace Jovanovich, 1993.

Krull, Kathleen and Kathryn Hewitt. *Lives of the Writers.* Harcourt Brace Jovanovich, 1994.

Fables

Aesop. *Aesop's Fables.* Harcourt Brace Jovanovich, 1992.

Demi. *Demi's Reflective Fables.* Grosset and Dunlap, 1988.

Lobel, Arnold. *Fables.* HarperTrophy, 1983.

Tompert, Ann. *Grandfather Tang's Story.* Crown, 1990.

Fairy Tales

French, Fiona. *Snow White in New York.* Oxford, 1990.

Louie, Ai-Ling (retold). *Yeh-Shen.* Philomel, 1982.

Scieszka, Jon. *The True Story of the Three Little Pigs.* Penguin Books, 1989.

Steptoe, John. *Mufaro's Beautiful Daughters.* Scholastic, 1987.

Vuong, Lynette Dyer. *The Brocaded Slipper.* HarperTrophy, 1982.

Wildsmith, Brian and Rebecca. *Jack and the Meanstalk.* Knopf, 1994.

Short Stories

Cherry, Lynne. *The Great Kapok Tree.* Harcourt Brace Jovanovich, 1990.

Polacco, Patricia. *Rechenka's Eggs.* Putnam, 1988.

Say, Allen. *Grandfather's Journey.* Houghton Mifflin, 1993.

Seuss, Dr. *The Lorax.* Random House, 1971.

Tall Tales

Kellogg, Steven. *Johnny Appleseed.* Morrow, 1988.

Kellogg, Steven. *Mike Fink.* Morrow, 1992.

Kellogg, Steven. *Paul Bunyan.* Morrow, 1984.

Kellogg, Steven. *Pecos Bill.* Morrow, 1987